Jordan
at the Big Game

Story by Jenny Giles   *Illustrations by Al Fiorentino*

CHILDREN!

Would you like to lead
one of the teams
onto the field today?

Put your name on your ticket.
Put your ticket into the red box.
You could be a lucky winner!

Jordan walked into the soccer stands
with his father.
"Look over there, Dad," he said.
"I'm going to put my ticket
into the box.
I could be one of the lucky winners."

"There will be a lot of names in that box," said Dad smiling.

"But I could still win," said Jordan.

CHILDREN!

Would you like to lead
one of the teams
onto the field today?

Put your name on your ticket.
Put your ticket into the red box.
You could be a lucky winner!

Jordan and his dad went to sit down.
They watched as a man
came out onto the field with the box.

He said to everyone,
"Now for the names of the winners!"
Then he pulled out a ticket.
"The first name is... Liam Rivers!"

"That's Liam from my school!"
said Jordan.
"He's my friend!"

Then the man said,
"And the second name is... Nicky Hill!"

Jordan watched the two children
running down the steps
and onto the field.
"I didn't get picked, Dad," he said.

"Maybe you will next time,"
said his father.

Everyone waited and waited.

"Where did Liam go?" asked Jordan.
"I can't see him."

"He will be putting on a team jersey,"
said his father.
"But he will have to hurry.
It's time for the game to start."

Just then the man on the field said,
"Sorry to keep you waiting,
but we are going to pick
another name from the box.
And it's... Jordan Wilson!"

"That's me!" shouted Jordan.

"So it is!" laughed his dad.
"Away you go!"

Jordan ran down the steps
and raced across the field.

Someone gave Jordan a team jersey
and he put it on.
Then he saw Liam
standing all by himself.

"I told them
that I can't do it," said Liam.
"I'm too scared to go out there.
My legs keep shaking."

Liam was trying not to cry,
and Jordan felt sorry for him.

"Come on, Liam," said Jordan.
"You can do it.
We can run onto the field together."

"Here, Jordan! You can take the ball,"
said one of the captains.
"Now, is everyone ready?"

"Yes," smiled Liam.

"I'm ready," said Nicky.

"Then let's go!" said the captain.

And everyone cheered
as the three children
ran onto the field
with the teams following them.